EXECUTIVE EDITORS
Sarah Galbraith, Alan Doan,
Jenny Doan, David Mifsud

MANAGING EDITOR
Natalie Earnheart

CREATIVE DIRECTOR
Christine Ricks

PHOTOGRAPHER
BPD Studios

CONTRIBUTING PHOTOGRAPHER
Katie Whitt

VIDEOGRAPHER
Jake Doan

DESIGNER & TECHNICAL WRITER
Linda Johnson

PROJECT DESIGN TEAM
Natalie Earnheart, Jenny Doan,
Sarah Galbraith

AUTHOR OF PATCHWORK MURDER
Steve Westover

CONTRIBUTING COPY WRITERS
Katie Mifsud, Jenny Doan, Camille Maddox,
Natalie Earnheart, Christine Ricks, Alan
Doan, Sarah Galbraith

COPY EDITOR
Geoff Openshaw

CONTRIBUTING PIECERS
Jenny Doan, Natalie Earnheart,
Stephen Nixdorf, Cassie Nixdorf

CONTRIBUTING QUILTERS
Bernice Kelly, Deloris Burnett, Jamey Stone,
Betty Bates, Emma Jensen, Sherry Melton,
Cassie Martin, Amber Weeks, Sandi Gaunce,
Daniela Kirk, Amy Gertz, Patty St. John, Mari
Zullig, Megan Gilliam, Lauren Dorton, Sam
Earnheart, Amber Wendt, Mary Bontrager

CONTACT US
Missouri Star Quilt Co
114 N Davis
Hamilton, Mo. 64644

content

HELLO
from MSQC

I love the Thanksgiving season. In the hustle and bustle of everyday life, sometimes the good things in our lives tend to go unnoticed. I think it does the heart good to take a moment to reflect on all those sweet little blessings.

Years ago we spent a few months living in my sister's basement. Because space was limited, each of us chose one or two special things to keep with us and everything else was put into storage. Alan chose his prized collection of baseball cards and I selected my guitars and an antique dresser that was very special to me. From family photos to childhood treasures, we were surrounded by only our most precious possessions, the things we thought that we just really couldn't live without.

Of course life has a funny way of showing us what really matters. During our stay in that basement, it flooded. Then it flooded again. Then again. My sister's basement had never before had so much as a drippy faucet, but in the hundred or so days that we stayed there it flooded five times! We lost everything. All of our most valued treasures, gone. It was devastating. It seemed that the whole family fell into a slump. We were sad. We were angry. It just wasn't fair.

So one day I took a brush and painted on the wall, "I AM THANKFUL FOR..." I hung a pen on a string and encouraged everyone to write down all the reasons we had to feel grateful. Every time someone walked by they would grab the pen and write on the wall. If they were feeling down, they'd write on the wall. When friends came over, they'd write on the wall, too. Pretty soon it was hard to find an empty space to write! We had this whole wall filled with all sorts of wonderful thankful things!

We discovered that in spite of what we had lost, we had so much to be thankful for. The things that really mattered were up on that wall and most of those, well, they weren't "things" at all.

Jenny

JENNY DOAN
MISSOURI STAR QUILT CO

"" We hope our magazine— BLOCK will inspire you to create beautiful quilts. ""

I'm Thankful For...

pencils, cards, Hot Choco, Seth, spices, snowboard

lants, Familytime, Fish, CLOUDS, Natalie, Holidays, Silly Jokes, Front Porches, Medicine, Electricity, Jo

ccoli, FOOTBALL, apple pie, Carrots, DiRT BiKes, Pumpkins, BALLOONS, GARDening, picnics, Crafts, Letters

musical instruments, SUGAR, BREAD, camping, Parties

Radio, Strawberries, SOFTBALL

Rugs, Neighbors, Sarah, Electric Blankets, Heaters, Fans, sewing machines, grandma, Bees, school, Singing

nksgiving, Snow Days!, chocolate, TV, Beds, Church, Rainbows, HORSES, woodworking, sweaters

Cake, Trees, FAMILY, Sunshine, BOOKS, glasses, Whistles, Pumpkin Pie, LAUGHTER, Friends, Se

SUNSHINE, Water, games, Cousins, SLe

Quilt

FABRIC, DAD, Flowers, Music, DOGS, Singing, Mountains, S,

Science, Love, Working, Cars, HUGS

Birthdays, Jenny, CATS, BONFIRES, Rain, SWIMMING, Smiles

Basketball, Teachers, Cookies, Drums, Ocean, MOM, Laughter, Jelly, Naptime!

School Supplies, Showers, Line Dancing, DANCING, RiVERS, Drum

king, Bus, Deoderant, Shoes, The park, Christmas, Trampoline, New Socks

Jackets, Summer, Bread, Alan

tics, Swimming, JOB, Back to School!, LIPS, Guitars, Sta

eyebrows, Technology, Bathtime, KIDS, Movies, Baseball, Grass

FiSH, T-shirts, MOON, Weddings, Pillows, Houses, Art, mor

SNOW, Ashelynn, SALAD Dressing, AMERICA, Bells, Air Conditioning, paper

Dogs, Imagination, SMILES, NOAH, Scissors, Cartwheels, Gideon, He

Friendship, lake, Annie

HARVEST *time*

Fall is upon us. The leaves are starting to turn jeweled tones of azure, gold and ruby red. Orange pumpkins and gourds are ready for the picking. Bright juicy red apples are falling off their branches and screaming to be made into tasty pies and cider. There exists an overabundance of sun-ripened tomatoes along with emerald zucchini and garden produce ready for soups, breads and any recipe we can come up with to use it all up.

I cherish these days spending time outside in the cool crisp air, then entering a warm house to its fragrant smells of wonderful concoctions cooking on the stove or baking in the oven.

Again, I find this palette of colors inspires me to create. I still have a little bit of time to whip up a couple new cozy quilts before the snow hits and we all just want to hibernate, right?

So, go bake a pie—or cook up a cozy quilt with this fall-inspired palette of color. Falling into some creativity can be easy when you are inspired by great colors and fabrics!

CHRISTINE RICKS
MSQC Creative Director, BLOCK MAGAZINE

SOLIDS

FBY13003 RJR Cotton Supreme Solids - Syrah
SKU-9617-324

FBY8527 RJR Cotton Supreme Solids - Mandarin
SKU-9617-159

FBY12977 RJR Cotton Supreme Solids - Night
SKU-9617-280

FBY13012 RJR Cotton Supreme Solids - Bougainvillea
SKU-9617-333

FBY8530 RJR Cotton Supreme Solids - Moss
SKU-9617-164

FBY8536 RJR Cotton Supreme Solids - Wimbledon
SKU-9617-205

PRINTS

FBY16071 Into the Woods - Bark
by Vanessa Goertzen for Moda Fabrics
SKU-5002 19

FBY15410 Indian Summer - Cottage Floral Coral
by Dover Hill for Benartex Studios
SKU-0077526B

FBY14326 Rustique - Yes Deer
by Emily Herrick for Michael Miller Fabrics
SKU-DC6409-NAVY-D

FBY13888 Midnight Gems - Maison Jewel
by Michael Miller Fabrics
SKU-PC6312-JEWE-D

FBY15051 Daily Zen - Pick Up Sticks Grass Green
by Michele D'Amore Designs for Benartex Fabrics
SKU-0173744B

FBY10475 Chantilly - Wall Flowers Dill
by Lauren & Jesse Jung for Moda Fabrics
SKU-25070 25

Snowballed pinwheel

quilt designed by NATALIE EARNHEART

To create this quilt, we took an ordinary pinwheel and made it extraordinary by just snowballing the corners. It's funny how one simple adjustment completely changes the entire design.

Last year, as a good friend awaited the arrival of her third child, a little boy due right at Thanksgiving time, she counted the days until she would finally be done with the discomforts of pregnancy. The birth was a cinch and my friend's heart was filled with contentment as she packed her things to leave the hospital and introduce her new tiny prince to the world.

And then it began. The very day that the baby came home from the hospital, the two- and four-year-olds came down with a nasty case of stomach flu. Then, the washing machine stopped working. The laundry from two sick toddlers and one new baby piled up quickly. Those first few days at home involved a lot of stress, a lot

> " It was a miracle, plain and simple. Her burdens seemed so much lighter when she began to realize how little of them she had actually been carrying by herself. "

of mess, three extremely needy children, along with very little sleep.

That was chapter one of a slew of difficulties—car problems, a stay at the hospital for the baby, who had contracted RSV, a tonsillectomy for the two year old, more car problems, and a never-ending stream of bills. It was pretty rough for a while but as the year went on, things settled down considerably and regular day-to-day life was able to resume its quiet pace.

Feeling finally in control but very battle scarred, my friend looked back on the events of the past few months. She was feeling pretty impressed with her ability to hold things to-gether, both emotionally and financially, despite the whirlwind

of difficulties they had faced. At the same time, though, she felt a good amount of self-pity and resentment.

Then, one day, while working on taxes with her husband, my friend was shocked to discover exactly how much had been spent that year on medical expenses alone. Of course they had struggled to pay bill after bill, but not until this moment had the total sum been calculated. It was much, much more than they should have possibly been able to afford. And yet they had done it.

That moment was a game changer for my friend. Certainly it had not been her own strict budgeting that had allowed them to pay all those bills. No amount of clever calculations could have allowed for that. Neither could it have been her own resiliency that had afforded her a good measure of peace and sanity during the tough times. It was a miracle, plain and simple. Her burdens seemed so much lighter when she began to realize how little of them she had actually been carrying by herself.

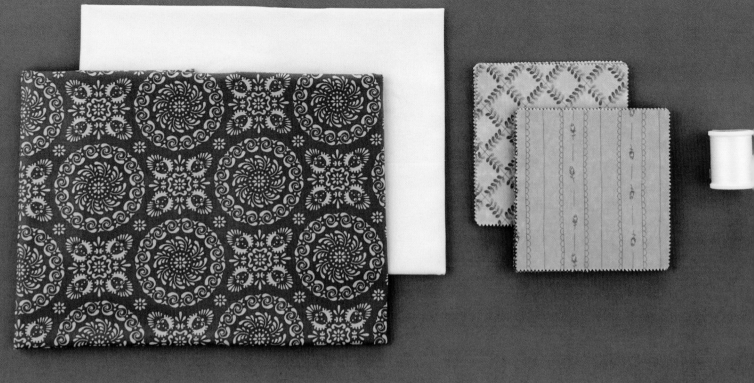

materials

makes a 50" X 60½" charm pack quilt

QUILT TOP
- 2 print charm packs
- 4 solid charm packs
- ¾ yd outer border

BINDING
- ½ yd coordinating fabric

BACKING
- 3¼ yds coordinating fabric

SAMPLE QUILT
- **Rambling Rose** by Sandy Gervais for Moda Fabrics
- **Bella Solids Snow (11)** by Moda Fabrics

1 sew

Pair two charm squares RST (right sides together)—one background solid, one print. Sew a ¼" seam around the edge.

You can stop and turn a quarter inch before the end or simply sew off the end—your choice. Sew all **but** 4 pairs; **Yield:** 80 pairs.

2 cut

Cut across the charm squares diagonally twice. Using a rotating cutting mat can make this step easier. Press seams to the dark side.

Yield: 4 HSTs/per pair (half square triangles).

1 pair up 1 print + 1 solid RST

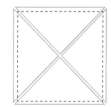

2 sew ¼" around outside edge; cut diagonally 2x

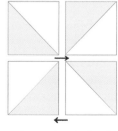

3A construct pinwheel

TIP: *Want to reduce bulk in the center AND ensure all pinwheel seams will nest as you sew blocks together? Unpick the last 2-3 stitches in the seam allowances of seams marked with X. Press remaining seams. If done correctly, a mini pinwheel will form in the seam allowances at the center.* **3B**

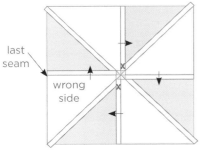

3B the background fabric of all seam allowances will be visible; all seams are pressed toward the print triangles

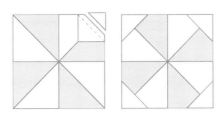

4A press a diagonal sewing line in the 2½" squares; sew, trim & press open
4B snowball all 4 corners

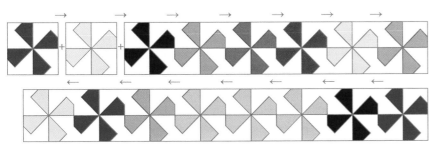

5 sew blocks together in rows; press seams in the same direction every other row

3 pinwheels

Arrange 4 HSTs of the same print to create a pinwheel. Follow the diagram: print, solid, print, solid. . .

Join the top 2 HSTs together; then the bottom 2 HSTs. Press all seams toward the print triangles. They should nest easily now as you join rows together. *(See TIP) Repeat steps 1-3 with all pairs. Square up the pinwheels so they are identical.

Block size: 5¾" x 5¾"
Yield: 80 blocks

4 snowball blocks

From the last solid charm packs, remove 4 squares. Cut the remaining charm squares (80) in half horizontally and vertically.

Yield: (320) 2½" solid squares.

Iron a diagonal crease into each solid square. Lay a square RST on a corner of the pinwheel. Sew on the crease across the small squares. Chain piecing will make this go quickly. Trim seam allowance to ¼" and press back. **4A** Repeat for all 4 corners of each block. **4B**

5 arrange & sew

Lay out blocks in an eye-pleasing fashion using an 8 x 10 setting. Sew blocks together side-by-side into rows. To ensure seams will nest when sewing rows together, press seams between blocks in even rows to the same side; in odd rows to the opposite side. Follow arrows. Join rows to complete the quilt center.

QUILT CENTER SIZE: 42½" x 53"

1 After sewing ¼" around the perimeter of a print/solid pair, cut diagonally twice to make (4) HSTs (half square triangles). Step 2.

2 Like a 4-patch join 2 HSTs at a time. See step 3.

3 Then join top and bottom pairs to complete the pinwheel. Step 3.

4 To snowball the block place a 2½" square on each corner, sew across, trim and press. Step 4.

A

C   D

B

6 borders

From the inner border fabric cut (6) 4″ strips. Follow steps in *construction basics* to attach to the quilt. **A-D** Press to the borders.

7 quilt & bind

Layer quilt top on batting and backing and quilt the way you like. Square up all raw edges.

Cut (6) 2½″ strips from binding fabric to finish. See *construction basics* for greater detail.

Teacup quilt

quilt designed by NATALIE EARNHEART

What could be cozier than sitting outside with a warm cup of tea on a beautiful autumn day? I just adore that kind of weather when there is a chilly little bite to the air but if you sit still enough to really soak in the sunshine, it is just enough to keep you warm. I love to sneak out early in the morning while everyone is still sleeping and the whole world is quiet and calm. Nothing is more peaceful than relaxing in my rocking chair on the front porch as I sip my tea and finish up a good book.

You know, a cup of tea is almost like a universal symbol for comfort and peace. Which is why you may be surprised that I've got a young friend who hates tea.

Yes, Karen hates tea, but she wants so badly to love it. You see, Karen adores everything about tea: the sweet little teacups and saucers, the adorable creamers and sugar bowls, even the itty bitty sandwiches that often accompany a cup of tea. In fact, Karen owns an extensive collection of beautiful tea sets and exotic teas. She hosts the best tea parties complete with delectable petit fours, fancy cupcake stands, and, best of all, silly nicknames like "Lady Cumberbatch."

teacup quilt

Whenever she is feeling under the weather Karen brews herself a pot of herbal tea. And yet, with each sip she takes from her carefully chosen floral teacup (with golden rim, of course), she shudders just a little as she forces it down.

Oh, the torture of being born a tea enthusiast with such a distaste for the stuff! I've suggested she just fill her teapot with hot chocolate or orange juice, but Karen refuses vehemently. She is very dedicated to her ill-fated love affair.

Fortunately for the rest of us tea-lovers, a nice little cup of tea is truly one of the sweet things of life—so simple, so relaxing, so peaceful—just like a favorite quilt.

The Teacup Quilt is everything its name suggests: super cute and wonderfully simple. As cozy as a warm cup of tea, it is sure to add a touch of charm to a chilly autumn morning spent admiring the beauty of the season.

materials

makes a 68" X 76½" layer cake quilt

QUILT TOP
- 1 print layer cake
- ½ yd inner border
- 1½ yds outer border

BINDING
- ½ yd coordinating fabric

BACKING
- 4¼ yds **OR** 2¼ yds 90" wide

SAMPLE QUILT
- **French Navy** by Studio 8 for Quilting Treasures

1 cut

Pair up all the fabrics in the layer cake. Right sides all facing up. Remember to cut and sew only one pair at a time. Cut your pairs as follows:

  A) 2" strip
  B) 3½" strip;
  C) subcut B: (2) 2" rectangles

2 sew

Swap out the **B** sections of your fabric pairs. Sew a contrasting **C** to both the top and bottom of **B**. Press to the dark side.

3 construct block

Sew **A** and **D** strips to either side of your

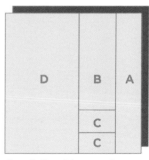

1 pair & cut layer cakes

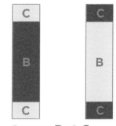

2 swap **B**s & **C**s

1 For this block to come together correctly, A, B/C, & D sections must be aligned evenly along the top. See step 3.

2 Remove the hanging tails. Now the block measures 9" x 9." Step 3.

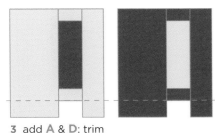

3 add **A** & **D**; trim

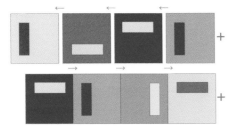

4 rotate & arrange blocks into rows
5 sew blocks into rows; then rows together to make the quilt center

 TIP: *Big bonus: no points to match! Just nest those seams between rows.*

B/C unit. **A**, **B/C** & **D** strips should line up evenly along the top edge. You will have tails! Cut the tails to square up the block.
Block size: 9" x 9"
Make 42.

4 arrange

Rotate and arrange blocks into a 6 x 7 grid. Using a design wall or your floor, will help you create the arrangement you like. This is where you decide which combinations you enjoy. No one will be arrested by any quilt police. . . so, go for it!

5 make quilt center

Sew blocks together starting at the top left and working across. RST attach each block to the next to make a row. Press seams to one side in the row; opposite side in the next row. Follow pressing arrows. Sew rows together nesting the pressed seams as you go.

Quilt Center: 51½" x 60"

 TIP: For more detail about adding borders, diagonal seams or attaching binding, see the construction basics section.

6 borders

Cut (7) 2½" strips from the inner border fabric. Measure the width of the quilt in 3 places to get an average. Cut 2 strips to that size, piecing if needed. Stitch one to the top edge RST. Border fabric should be on top as you sew to reduce wavy borders. Press to the border. Repeat for the bottom edge. Follow the same procedure for the sides. Include the newly attached top & bottom borders in your measurements.

For the outer borders cut (7) 6½" strips and follow the same process used for attaching inner borders.

7 quilt & bind

Layer and quilt the way you like. Square up the quilt. Cut (8) 2½" strips and piece together end-to-end using the plus sign method of making diagonal seams. Fold lengthwise WST and attach to the quilt edge. Finish by hand or machine. Voilà!

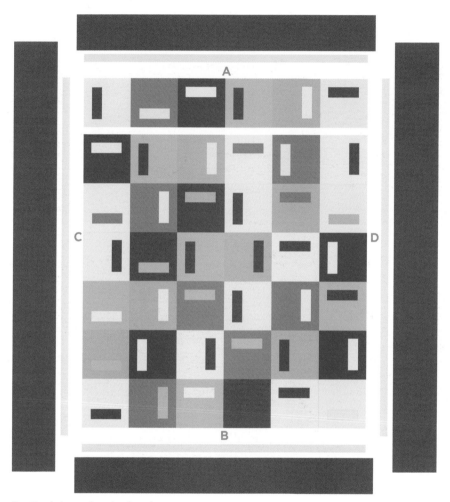

6 attach inner & outer borders

Hexagon
braid

table runner designed by NATALIE EARNHEART

Whenever I see this table runner, I think of my little girls and their braids. Every morning, when my girls were small, we gathered in the bathroom to do hair. The girls loved all different kinds of styles, and I have to say, they really thought they were quite fashionable! But braids were almost always their preferred style. We learned to make french braids, braids down the back, fishtail braids, braids that wound around or along the sides of the head, you name it! The girls would even braid their hair onto wires so the braids could be bent into any shape or design they wanted! Being creative with my girls hair is a cherished and lasting memory.

A braid is such a simple thing: three small sections that are woven together to create a beautiful, strong whole. I like to think of my three girls as sections of a braid. Each wonderful in her own right, but over time they have become knitted together as tightly and solidly as one of their expertly plaited braids. Individually, they are incredible but together, they are unstoppable.

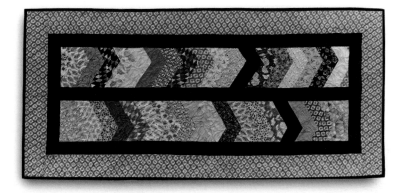

I am certain that the time the girls spent together crammed into that little bathroom braiding each other's hair was integral in forming the special bonds they now share. Those simple moments are what gradually create relationships that last a lifetime.

Now that my daughters are grown and have little girls of their own, the braiding tradition lives on. It is so fun to have my granddaughters come to visit with their beautiful hair styled in an ever-changing variety of cute ways. Of course, in hair styles as in quilting, the possibilities are endless. And with all the fun ideas available online, I have a feeling they won't run out of creative new styles for many years to come!

We all have a spark of creativity within us, and there's just nothing as fun as letting your imagination take your ideas to totally new places. I love the new spin on the braid in this table runner. Make one simple change and you have created a completely different design! Why settle for the same old style day after day when there are so many fabulous new ideas just waiting to be created?

THE HEXAGON BRAID LOOKS GORGEOUS in a variety of colors and fabrics. You can use up your scraps, or that charm pack you've been holding on to. A table runner is a beautiful way to dress up your table!

“ I love the new spin on the braid in this table runner. Make one simple change and you have created a completely different design! ”

materials

makes a 24½" x 52½" charm pack table runner

TABLE RUNNER TOP
- 1 print 5"charm pack
- ½ yd solid for sashing/inner border
- ½ yd outer border

BINDING
- ½ yd coordinating fabric

BACKING
- 1¾ yds coordinating fabric

SAMPLE TABLE RUNNER
- **Persimmon** by BasicGrey for Moda Fabrics

1 cut

Cut all charm squares in half once. Use the hexagon template and cut a hexagon shape from each 2½" x 5" rectangle.

Yield: (84) hexagons

2 begin a braid

To begin a braid lay 2 hexagons of the same print into position. The side of one hexie abuts the bottom of another. **2A**

Flip the bottom hexie to the wrong side and match the edges leaving a dog ear at the beginning. Sew the short seam. **2B**

3 build the braid

From this point forward the bottom of

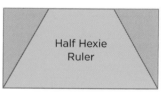

Half Hexie Ruler

1 cut half hexie shapes from half charm squares; 2 from each square

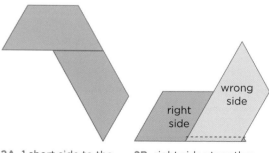

2A 1 short side to the other hexie's long bottom side

right side

wrong side

2B right sides together, sew the half seam

3A the bottom of the next hexie crosses the seam

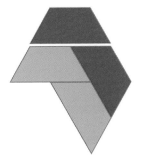

3B add 2 hexies of the same print one after another.

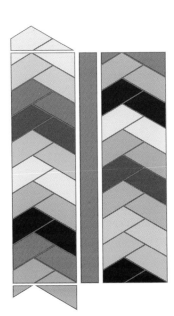

4 trim & add sashing between braids

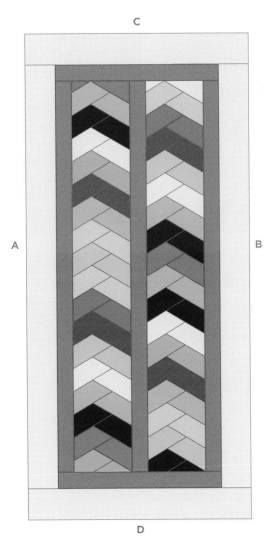

the next hexie will *always* cross the seam just sewn. **3A**

Continue in this fashion always adding 2 hexies of the same print one after another. **3B** This will give the quilt the angled striped look.

Repeat with 21 pairs of same print hexies.

Make 2 braids.

4 sashing & borders

Trim the top & bottom of both braids. They must be equal in length. Cut (1) 2½″ WOF strip of sashing and join the 2 braids.

Quilt center size: 14″ x 42″

From the inner border fabric cut (3) 2½″ strips. Follow steps in *construction basics* to attach to the quilt. **A-D** *(Note: attach sides first for this project)* Press to the borders.

Cut (4) 3½″ strips of outer border fabric. Attach to the quilt in the same manner as the inner border.

5 quilt & bind

Layer quilt top on batting and backing and quilt the way you like. Square up all raw edges.

Cut (4) 2½″ strips from binding fabric to finish. See *construction basics* for greater detail.

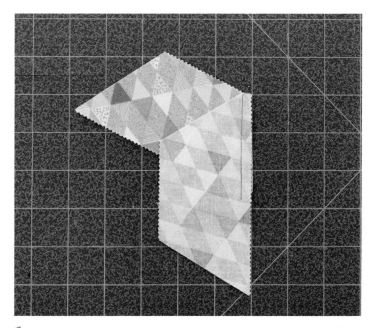

1 Sew the short seam of the first braid pair. See 2B.

2 Add 2 hexagons of the same print. Notice how the previous seam is crossed each time a new hexagon is added. See 3A & B

3 Trim the braid at the bottom leaving a straight edge. Line the ruler up to the braid's straight sides. See step 4.

4 Trim the top in the same manner as the bottom. Remember both braids need to be the same length. See step 4.

Triangle
tango

quilt designed by NATALIE EARNHEART

I love a bargain. I know it's a little silly but I get quite a thrill from scoring a great deal. Sometimes I'll walk into the living room with a bag full of purchases and proudly announce, "Guess how much I paid for this?"

"A million bucks?" my husband will often joke.

"Thirty-six bucks! Thirty-six bucks for two hundred and sixty-five dollars worth of stuff!!!"

"Great!" he'll reply, and then add with a wink, "Do we need two hundred and sixty-five dollars worth of stuff?"

"Are you kidding? At this price, I probably should have gotten two of everything!"

Even though he teases, he really does appreciate the

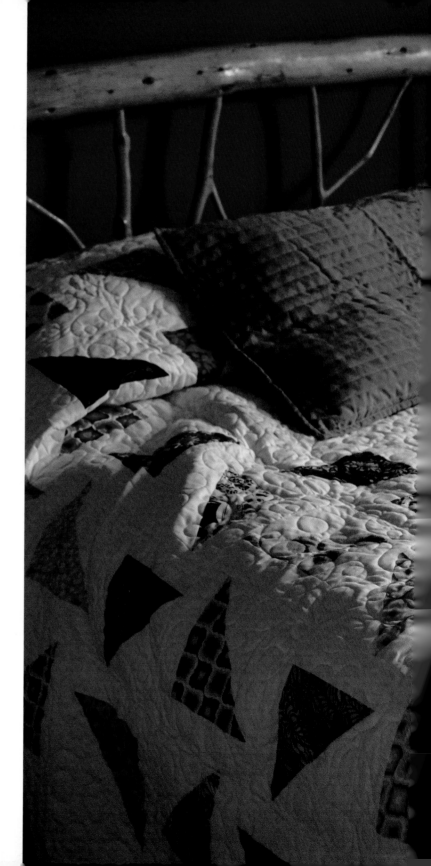

way I know how to stretch a dollar. When the kids were young, it was quite the task to get everyone outfitted with new clothes for school, but I loved the challenge. It was during those years that I developed an almost superhuman ability to sniff out the very best bargains. When I combined my finely-honed deal-finding skills with the small budget we had set aside for back-to-school shopping, I did a pretty good job providing each kid with a sufficient ward-robe of nice things to wear. Of course, when you're out to find a good deal, name-brand anything is just not a luxury that comes along often.

I remember a year when one of the boys wanted a pair of designer jeans. I explained to him that if he got those top-dollar jeans, that would be pretty much the only new clothing he would get for school that year. Still, he insisted that he had to have those jeans, so we got them. When school started, my son felt pretty cool in his new expen-sive jeans. That is, until he saw all of the nice things his brothers and sisters had to choose from. While the other kids had a fairly good assortment of things to wear, my son was stuck with only his fancy pants

and whatever still fit him from the previous school year. It was a hard lesson to learn, but I think he really came to understand what it means to be a good steward over the money that you have been given.

Now that the kids are all grown, they too have become well-seasoned bargain hunters. We all work hard to make the most of the things with which we have been blessed.

One of the reasons that I love this quilt so much is that with just two layer cakes and some yardage you can make a quilt large enough for a king size bed. You don't have to skimp on style to create a huge quilt at a great price. These principles of economy apply not just to quilting, but also to back-to-school shopping, grocery shopping, and anything, really. All it takes is a little creativity to make the most out of any situation!

materials

makes a 113" X 97" layer cake quilt

QUILT TOP
- 1 print layer cake
- 1 solid layer cake
- 5 yds solid yardage **OR** 2 solid jelly rolls (same solid as the layer cakes)

BINDING
- 1 yd coordinating fabric

BACKING
- 8¾ yds **OR** 3½ yds 108" wide

SAMPLE QUILT
- **Moonshine** by Tula Pink for Free Spirit Fabrics
- **Arctic White** by Free Spirit Fabrics

1 sew

Pair two layer cake squares—one background solid, one print—RST (right sides together). Sew a ¼" seam around the edge.

You can stop and turn a quarter inch before the end or simply sew off the end, it's your choice.

2 cut

Cut across the layer cakes diagonally twice. Do not move the block between cuts. If possible, use a rotating cutting mat to make this step easier. Press seams to the dark side. Square up to 6½."

Yield: 4 HSTs (half square triangles)
Block size: 6½" x 6½"

1 pair up 1 print + 1 solid RST

2 sew ¼" around outside edge; cut diagonally 2x

3A yield: 4x HST; square up to 6½"

1 Once you've sewn the pairs together, cut them in half twice diagonally. See step 2.

2 To add sashing, begin by attaching a 6½" rectangle to one side of a print triangle. See 3B.

3 Add the 8½" sashing rectangle to the other print side of the triangle. See 3C.

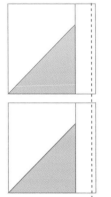
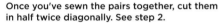

3B chain piece a 6½" rectangle to one side of the print triangle

3 add sashing

You will need (70) 2½" WOF strips either from jelly rolls or cut from background fabric. From these strips, subcut:

(28) WOF into 6½" rectangles.
(42) WOF into 8½" rectangles.

Yield: 168 of each size rectangle

Basically the sashing will frame the 90° corner of the print triangle. **3D**

Start by attaching a 6½" rectangle to a "print" side of the HST block. **3B**

Chain piecing will speed up this step. Feed an HST block and a 6½" rectangle RST through the sewing machine using a ¼" seam. Continue sewing off the fabric a few stitches then feed the next block + rectangle sashing through the machine and so on. Snip threads to separate blocks. Press to the sashing.

Repeat, adding the 8½" rectangle to the other print side of the HST block. **3C**

Block size: 8½" x 8½"

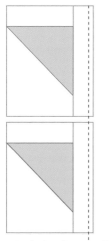

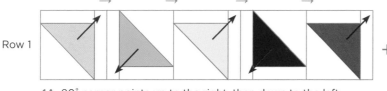

3D the sashing rectangles will frame the 90° corner of the print triangle

3C chain piece an 8½″ rectangle to the adjacent side

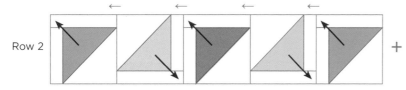

Row 1

4A 90° corner points up to the right, then down to the left

Row 2

4B 90° corner points up to the left, then down to the right

4 arrange & sew

The blocks are arranged in 2 basic alternating rows. Each row begins with the 90° print corner pointing up followed by the 90° print corner pointing down. For example, if the first block points up to the right, the second will point down to the left and so on. **4A** & **4B** Continue the sequence across and down.

Lay out all blocks with an eye to achieving an overall mix of light & dark color values in a 14 x 12 setting. Sew blocks together side-by-side into rows. Note the pressing arrows. Join rows to complete the quilt center. Nest seams as you go.

Quilt center size: 112½″ x 96½″

5 quilt & bind

Layer quilt top on batting and backing and quilt the way you like. Square up all raw edges.

Cut (8) 2½″ strips from binding fabric to finish. See *construction basics* for greater detail.

Jelly roll race 3

quilt designed by NATALIE EARNHEART

Every year about this time, geese start migrating south
to their winter homes. And yet it almost always catches
me off guard. I'll be out in the garden or at a little league
game gleefully enjoying my summer, when suddenly
the sky is filled with a flurry of flapping and honking
as a flock of geese races by in a perfect V. It seems to
happen before I've even really realized that summer has
come to a close. Those beautiful birds bring with them
such a sense of anticipation—fall is coming, and winter
isn't far behind.

I've often wondered how the geese know when to start
flying. While the rest of us are still focused on long, easy
days of sunshine, something whispers to those geese,
"Better get going! It's time!"

That rush of excitement as they pass overhead is echoed
in the brisk nature of the fall season. I feel such energy
and freshness as we trade the hot summer sun for those
little bites of frost on crunchy leaves. Even as the earth is
slowly falling asleep for winter, it seems like everything is

filled with one last burst of life—the smells, the colors, the clean, crisp air—all is bright and exciting.

One of my favorite fall time memories is of a visit we made to the mountains in early October. The leaves were brilliant shades of yellow, red and gold. We rode a ski lift up as far as it would take us and then got off and climbed another mile or so to the summit. There we sat, red-faced and breathing hard, looking out over the valley below us. It's funny how, sitting at the top of a mountain, you can feel all at once as large as life and also small and insignificant. The beauty that surrounded us was so breathtaking I was almost overwhelmed trying

to take it all in. The color, the cool air, the fresh scent of pine needles and dirt. It was truly awe-inspiring. I decided in that moment that fall would always be my favorite season.

Now, when I see those geese rushing by in such a hurry at the very beginning of fall, I think to myself, "Slow down, little birdies, you're about to miss the best part!"

materials

makes a 66½" X 77½" jelly roll quilt

QUILT TOP
- 1 jelly roll
- 1 yd solid for inner border & triangles
- 1¼ yds outer border

BINDING
- ¾ yd coordinating fabric

BACKING
- 4¼ yds 45" wide **OR** 2¼ yds 90" wide

SAMPLE QUILT
- **Lily's Garden Spice** by Patrick Lose for RJR
- **Cream** by Cotton Supremes for RJR

1 on your mark . . .

Open your jelly roll carefully leaving the strips in tact just as they come off the roll.

For the connecting triangles, cut (5) 2½" strips from the solid fabric. Subcut into (39) 4½" rectangles.

2 get ready . . .

Start with a jelly roll strip. Remove selvages. With the end of a JR (jelly roll) strip lying face up horizontally in front of you, place a 4½" rectangle on top at a 90° angle, lining up the sides and bottom. **2A** The sewing line will run from left to right, bottom to top (finger press a crease to sew on if you want). **2B** Trim off the corner a ¼" from the stitching line; press. **2C**

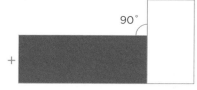

2A place a solid rectangle at the end of a JR strip RST at 90°; align bottoms and sides

2B sewline runs left to right; bottom to top; trim

2C press

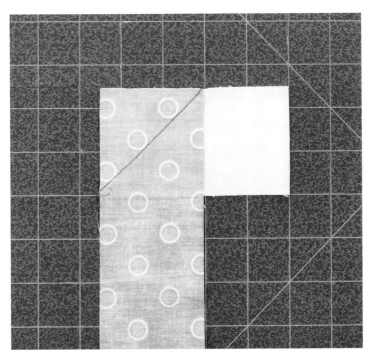

1 Alternate view of first seam. Use whichever view makes more sense to you. See 2A

2 Trim away the excess fabric. See 2B

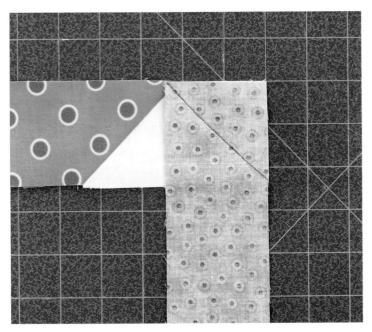

3 Add the next strip. It aligns to the top and right side of the white rectangle. The sewline runs top left to bottom right. See 3A & B.

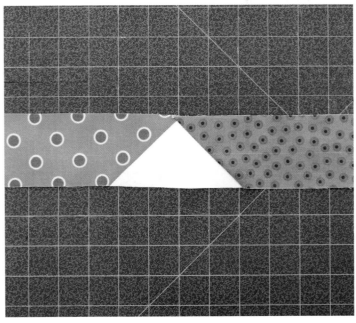

4 View of a finished flying geese strip. See 3C.

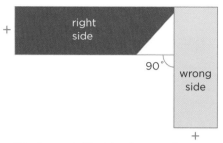

3A the next JR strip aligns to the top and side of the previous strip

3B sew left to right, top to bottom; trim & press

3C the triangle is formed

4 cut the fold before sewing completely to the end

3 get set . . .

Lay the strip + solid rectangle horizontally in front of you right side facing up. Lay the second JR strip face down this time aligning top and side to the solid rectangle. **3A** The seam will again run from left to right but this time, from top to bottom. **3B** You may want to finger press a sewing line for yourself. Trim excess and press. **3C**

Continue steps 2 & 3 until all the JR strips have been used. Remember to remove all selvages beforehand.

Yield: one continuous strip

Cut about 18″ off the last strip.
It really doesn't matter the exact measurement. This ensures the triangles will not end up on the edge of the quilt center.

4 sew!

Now the fun begins! Get to your sewing machine and . . . hold on to the end. Find the other end of your continuous strip. With both ends RST sew the strip to itself *lengthwise* all the way back to the fold. Go! Don't worry about twisting.

When you are close to the end, cut the fold, undoing any twist, and finish sewing. You've got 2 strips sewn together!

Again hold the end (now 2 strips wide), find the beginning and stitch RST lengthwise back to the fold. Cut the fold again. You've got 4 rows sewn together! Continue

in this fashion, 5 times total: 32 strips wide. Voilà! A quilt top. Press & square up.

Quilt Center: 51″ x 62″

5 borders

From the inner border fabric cut (6) 2½″ strips. Follow steps in *construction basics* to attach to the quilt. **A-D** Press to the borders.

Cut (7) 6″ strips of outer border fabric. Attach to the quilt in the same manner as the inner border.

6 quilt & bind

Layer quilt top on batting and backing and quilt the way you like. Square up all raw edges.

Cut (8) 2½″ strips from binding fabric to finish. See *construction basics* for greater detail.

A

C  D

diagram not an exact representation   B

Serendipity
I & II

quilt designed by JENNY DOAN

Serendipity means, "a fortunate happenstance or pleasant surprise." When I designed the Serendipity quilts, I was trying to create a block based on a more difficult quilt I had seen. As I worked, I noticed that I was creating a lot of waste—and you probably know that I hate waste—so I kept experimenting. Soon I realized that with the addition of one more seam, I would get a whole new block. Naturally, I tried to put the two blocks together in the same quilt, but it just didn't look right. That's when the light bulb came on! I decided that I could make two quilts that look completely different out of one block. What started out as a quest to recreate one quilt ended up as the creation of two completely new quilt designs. Serendipity!

I've had other serendipitous experiences in my life, and they've all been surprising and memorable. I remember when I first went to college, a group of friends were hanging out at my place. It just happened to be the birthday of one of the girls, and we all wanted to celebrate with some birthday cake. Miraculously, between the four of us we were able to round up cake mix, oil and eggs. (In a group of college freshmen, what are the chances of finding more than a few frozen pizzas?)

It wasn't until the cake batter was mixed and the oven preheated that we realized none of us had a cake pan! The evening seemed doomed to failure and we were almost resigned to just licking the beaters and calling it a night when a stroke of genius changed my life forever.

"Can't we just cook it in the waffle iron?", one of us asked. Cake cooked in the waffle iron? Can you do that? Will it work? Will it burn on the outside and stay all gooey in the middle? Given that we had no other options, we decided to give the waffle iron a go. I carefully spooned some of the batter into the iron. We closed the lid and waited. Soon the room filled with the heavenly scent of cake, which seemed like a very promising sign.

CREATIVE QUILTING IS ONE OF THE MOST fulfilling things I've ever done. These two quilts show how just a little bit of creativity can go a long way. The act of creating a quilt, and then getting a bonus quilt is pure joy!

When the moment finally came to open the waffle iron and check out our cake, we were delighted to find a perfectly cooked waffle-cake, hot and delicious. We had just baked a cake, and we had done it in less than five minutes without a pan or oven.

The waffle cake was one of the greatest inventions of my young life. Born of desperation, it was a delightful success that we had never dreamed of inventing. As pleasant a surprise as the creation of the Serendipity Quilts, waffle cake will forever hold a special place in my memory. After all, what is more fun than discovering something you never knew you were looking for in the first place?

" What started out as a quest to recreate one quilt ended up as the creation of two completely new quilt designs. Serendipity! "

materials

makes a 58" X 64" jelly roll quilt

QUILT TOP
- 1 print jelly roll
- 2½ yds background fabric
- 1 yd outer border

BINDING
- ½ yd coordinating fabric

BACKING
- 3¾ yds coordinating fabric

SAMPLE QUILT
- **Singapore Sling** by Stonehenge for Northcott Studio
- **Stonehenge Cream** by Stonehenge for Northcott Studio

1 sew strips

Sew 3 JR strips of various values together lengthwise: light, dark, medium. Press to the dark fabric.

Make (12) strip sets

2 cut blocks

Measure the width. Cut square blocks to that measurement from the strip sets. Our blocks measured 6½" square.

Yield: 72 blocks.

Important: stack the blocks with the light strip at the bottom.

1 make 12 strip sets
2 cut strip sets into 6½" squares & stack with light strip on the bottom

3A iron a diagonal crease in each 5" background square

3B position the 5″ square on the block; sew on the crease & ¼″ away

3C cut between stitching lines; set the waste block aside

3D repeat on opposite corner

3E final block: consistency is important

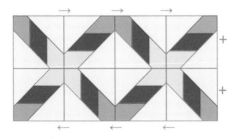

4 turn either the light or medium strips toward the center to reveal a friendship star in every 4-block group

From the background fabric cut:
(18) 5″ WOF strips; subcut into (144) 5″ squares

3 stitch & flip

Iron a diagonal crease into each 5″ square. This will be the first sewing line. **3A**

Place the square on a corner so that the crease connects adjacent sides. Sew on the ironed crease. Turn the block and sew ½″ away from the first seam line—closer to the corner. **3B**

With a rotary cutter cut between the 2 sewing lines. Set the smaller block aside; it can be used to make the *Serendipity II* quilt. Press corner out. **3C**

Repeat the stitch & flip technique on the block's opposite corner. **3D**

Consistency is important! Each block must show light strip bottom left, medium strip top right. **3E**

Make 72 blocks total.
Block size: 6½″ x 6½″

4 arrange & sew

Arrange blocks in an 8 x 9 setting. Turn them so either the medium or light fabric of the original strip set faces toward the center of every 4-block group. Once you've chosen medium or light to the center, repeat that orientation with the rest of the blocks. A friendship star appears in the center.

Sew blocks together to build rows first. Press seams to the same side every other row. Then sew rows together to complete the quilt center. Nest seams as you go.

Quilt Center Size: 48½″ x 54½″

5 outer border

From the outer border fabric cut (6) 5″ strips. Follow steps in *construction basics* to attach to the quilt. **A-D** Press to the borders.

6 quilt & bind

Layer quilt top on batting and backing and quilt the way you like. Square up all raw edges.

Cut (7) 2½″ strips from binding fabric to finish. See *construction basics* for greater detail.

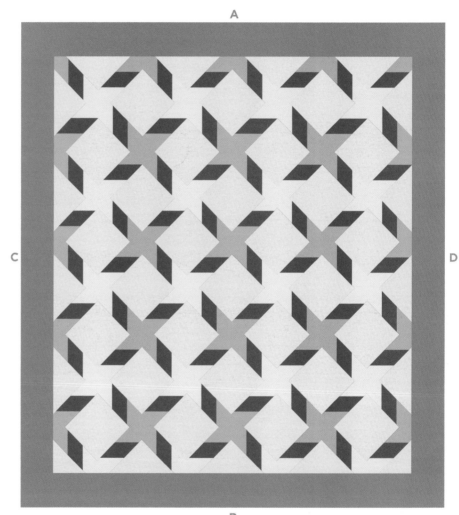

54

1 Subcut the strips sets into 6½" squares. See step 2.

2 Sew 2 seams: the first on the creased fold, the second ½" away toward the corner. See 3B.

3 Cut between the 2 seams. See 3C.

4 The resulting blocks after adding both 5" squares and cutting: 1 diagonal stripped block for Serendipity I (left) & 2 cast off HSTs for Serendipity II.

5 Every set of (4) 6½" blocks will reveal a friendship star. Turn the same fabric strip toward the center. See step 4.

6 Four of the cast off blocks will become a pinwheel for Serendipity II. See step 2, page 56.

Serendipity II

materials

makes a 55" X 55" jelly roll quilt

QUILT TOP
- (144) 4½" cast off blocks
- ¾ yd outer border

BINDING
- ½ yd coordinating fabric

BACKING
- 3½ yds coordinating fabric

SAMPLE QUILT
- **Singapore Sling** by Stonehenge for Northcott Studio
- **Stonehenge Cream** by Stonehenge for Northcott Studio

1 cast off block from *Serendipity I*

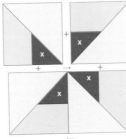

2 build the block like a 4-patch; sew rows together first; press seams according to arrows; then sew top & bottom together

1 square up

Square up the cast-off blocks left over from *Serendipity I* to 4½" squares. Remove any portion of a 3rd strip in the seam allowance.

2 build the block

If possible, use 4 blocks that have the same print triangle top to build a block. Note the triangles with an "x" displayed. Arrange blocks to form a pinwheel—a larger background triangle separates each "x" triangle.

Sew the blocks together in rows first. Press seams in opposite directions. Then sew the 2 rows together nesting the middle seam.

Yield: 36 blocks
Block size: 8" x 8"

3 press pinwheels

There is a way to reduce bulk in pinwheel blocks AND ensure all seams are "nestable" as you sew blocks together.

Flip the pinwheel block to the wrong side. *Ignore all diagonal seams.* Concentrate on the seams that extend to the block's sides. Locate the last seam sewn. The 2 seams that were crossed by the last seam are the ones to focus on. Those are marked as "X."

In their seam allowances ONLY, unpick the last 2-3 stitches. They should already be pressed in opposite directions. Once the stitches are removed, the last seam can be pressed in opposite directions—toward the prints. If done correctly, a mini pinwheel will form in the seam allowances at the center.

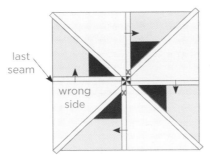

3 once complete, all seams are pressed toward the print triangles

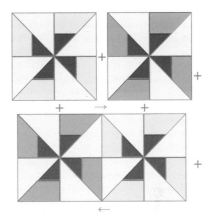

4 sew blocks into rows first; then rows together to make the quilt center

4 arrange & sew

Arrange blocks in an 6 x 6 setting. Sew blocks together to build rows first. Press seams to the same side every other row. Then sew rows together to complete the quilt center. Nest seams as you go.

Quilt Center Size: 45½" x 45½"

5 outer border

From the outer border fabric cut (5) 5" strips. Follow steps in *construction basics* to attach to the quilt. **A**-**D** Press to the borders.

6 quilt & bind

Layer quilt top on batting and backing and quilt the way you like. Square up all raw edges.

Cut (6) 2½" strips from binding fabric to finish. See *construction basics* for greater detail.

Sidewalk chalk

quilt designed by NATALIE EARNHEART

When I was a little girl, Mary Poppins was my very favorite movie. And everyone knows that the best part of the whole show is the magical chalk drawing scene. You know the one, right? Mary Poppins grabs hold of the children's hands and they all hop together into an enchanted adventure inside a chalk drawing on the sidewalk near the park. Of course, anything is possible when you are inside a drawing: magical merry-go-round horse races, dancing and singing with barnyard animals, afternoon tea served by penguins. There's really no limit! What could be more fun?!

So when our family moved to a small town called Spreckels, I was delighted to discover that at certain times of the year artists came and drew different scenes on the big sidewalk that circled the town's central park. From African plains with tall yellow grass to mysterious, deep, green forests, these beautiful scenes sparked my young imagination. How I longed to jump into those drawings and see what there was to see!

Even now, I sometimes daydream of breaking out the ol' sidewalk chalk and sketching for myself a nice, quiet spot with a hammock and a good book. Then maybe, just maybe, if I close my eyes and wish hard enough, I could hop right in and take a little break from life! (If not, I could at least draw a circle around myself with a 100-foot radius and the words, "Do not enter! This crazy lady needs some peace!")

I'm sure most of us would love the chance to escape reality for an hour or two and just romp around in a fantasy land of our own imagining. Would you go swimming through the warm, turquoise waters of the Caribbean? Spend some time quilting in a magical sewing room outfitted with floor to ceiling shelves of fabric as far as the eye can see? Go hog-wild in a gourmet cupcake shop with a "FREE" sign on the door? (Hey, your fantasy, your rules!) Maybe your dream scene would be a much simpler place. Maybe your wish would be for nothing more than a peaceful afternoon spent with dear ones.

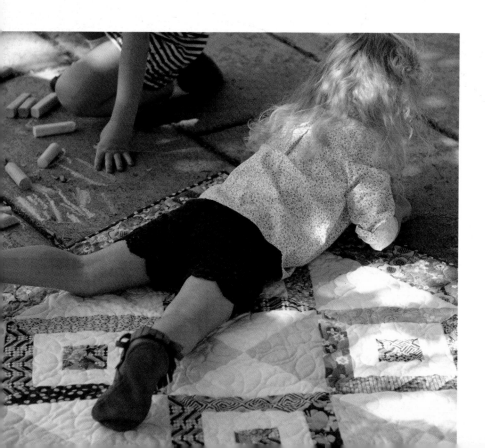

When we designed this quilt and Natalie decided to name it "Summer in the Park," I immediately thought back to that park in Spreckels and all those wonderful chalk drawings. "Summer in the Park" is as beautiful and idyllic as those happy days I spent in Spreckels dreaming of magical adventures. What I didn't realize as a child was that I didn't really need magical adventures in imaginary lands; that sweet little park in the center of our quiet town was already about as close to heaven as it gets.

materials
makes a 106" X 90" jelly roll quilt

QUILT TOP
- 1 print jelly roll
- 2 yds solid background
- 3¼ yds white background
- 1½ yds outer border

BINDING
- ¾ yd coordinating fabric

BACKING
- 8¼ yds **OR** 3¼ yds 108" wide

SAMPLE QUILT
- **Glow** by Amy Bulter for Rowan
- **Bella Breeze (132)** by Moda Fabrics
- **Bella Solids White (98)**
  by Moda Fabrics

1 make strip sets

From the white background fabric, cut (20) 2½" WOF strips.

Use (2) 2½" print strips and sandwich 1 white WOF strip between them. Stitch all 3 together lengthwise with a ¼" seam.

Yield: 1 strip set
Make 20 strip sets total.

2 make tubes

The width of each strip set should measure 6½." From the background white AND the background solid fabrics cut (10) 6½" WOF strips each.

Pair these fabric strips RST with the 20

1 sandwich 1 white WOF strip between 2 print 2½" strips = 1 strip set

2A pair each strip set with a 6½" background fabric strip

2B sew ¼" along both lengthwise edges, making a tube

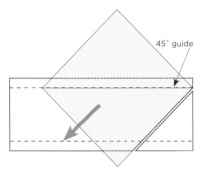

3A the 45° ruler guideline rests on the top line of stitching; the ruler's far right corner is at the tube's edge; cut and slide down following the cut edge

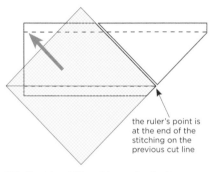

the ruler's point is at the end of the stitching on the previous cut line

3B line the 45° guide to the bottom line of stitching; cut, then slide the ruler up along the newly cut edge

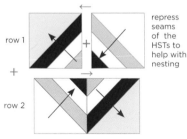

repress seams of the HSTs to help with nesting

row 1

row 2

4 arrange white & solid HSTs; sew blocks together in rows; then rows together to make a final block.

strip sets: 10 paired with solid, 10 paired with white. **2A**

Sew pairs right sides together lengthwise along both edges to make a tube. **2B**

3 cut

Use a ruler with a 45° guideline that has sides long enough to span the diagonal width of the tube—at least 9½." Line up the 45° line to the seam at the top. Make the first cut. Toss the scrap. **3A**

Next slide the ruler down to the bottom line of stitching, moving along the cut edge of fabric. Make the second cut when the ruler's 45° guideline sits on the stitching.
1 block cut. **3B**

Now return to the top line of stitching, moving the ruler along the newly cut edge. Continue in this fashion with all the strip tubes. Make 60 white & 60 solid HSTs.

Yield: 6 HSTs per strip set
Block size: 8½" x 8½" (Square up)

4 make blocks

To make nesting seams easier, press all the seams of the white HSTs to the center; seams of all the solid HSTs to the outside. Arrange 2 white & 2 solid HSTs as shown.

Sew blocks in rows first. Press seams in opposite directions. Then sew the 2 rows together. Make 30.

Block size: 16½" x 16½"

5 arrange & sew

Lay the blocks into a 6 x 5 grid. All blocks are oriented with a white HST in the upper right hand corner. Sew blocks together in rows; then rows together. Press seams in opposite directions from row to row.

Quilt Center Size: 96½" x 80½"

6 borders

From the outer border fabric cut (10) 5" strips. Follow steps in *construction basics* to attach to the quilt. **A-D** Press to the borders.

7 quilt & bind

Layer quilt top on batting and backing and quilt the way you like. Square up all raw edges.

Cut (10) 2½" strips from binding fabric to finish. See *construction basics* for greater detail on how to create and attach binding.

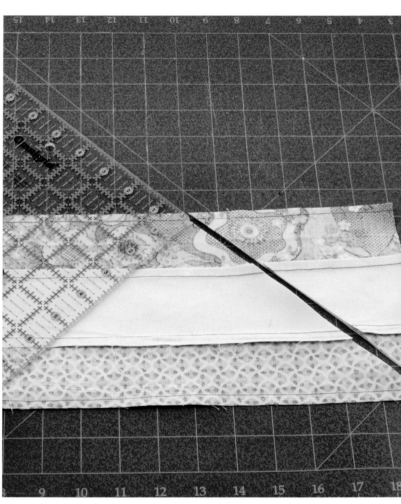

1 You can start with the top or the bottom line of stitching. The ruler's 45 degree line rests on the stitching line. Make the first cut. See 3A.

2 Slide the ruler to the top line of stitching. Notice how the ruler continues the angle of the first cut. See 3A & B.

C

A  B

D

Rag Quilt

designed by JENNY DOAN

Many moons ago, when I had only eleven grandchildren,
I decided to make a quilt for each of them for Christmas.
Because I was making so many, I needed to choose a quilt
that was easy, not too expensive, and could be completed
quickly. When I heard about the Rag Quilt technique, I knew
I had found the perfect quilt idea!

I carefully selected a variety of different flannels. I wanted
something that would be special to each child, from my
perfectly-pink princess to my nothing-but-sports little
buddy. With the fabric organized, I began cutting and sewing
squares. The quilts came together quickly and soon all I had
left to do was clip the edges to create the ragged border.
Easy, right? Wrong.

Back then, rag snips had not yet been invented and I had to
cut each and every little piece of fringe with a pair of scissors.
Pretty soon I had blisters, but Christmas just kept getting
closer so I layered on the bandages and kept going.

I can't remember a time that my hands ached as much as
they did clipping all those blankets, but all that pain disap-

peared the moment I saw the happy looks on my sweet grandkids' faces that Christmas. As they unwrapped their new quilts and chattered excitedly about the different flannels, I knew that I had done a wonderful thing. It warmed my heart to see those kids so cozy and content in their special new quilts. But as I glanced down at my weary, bandaged hands, I vowed I would never do it again. . . that is, until rag snips were invented!

There is something so special about receiving handcrafted gifts. Knowing the time and effort that went into a gift adds a layer of love and appreciation that you can't buy at any store. I remember when my kids were little, how proud they would be to present me with macaroni necklaces and hand-drawn greeting cards. How I treasured those sweet little gifts! They may not have sparkled like a new pair of diamond earrings, but my maternal heart would swell to almost bursting to think of the love my tiny ones had put into my simple gifts.

By the same token, I really love being able to give gifts that I have made. I feel like when a loved one wraps up in one of my quilts, it's almost like they are wrapped up in one of my famous hugs.

This rag quilt really is a wonderful choice to make for a quick and easy gift that will be cherished for years to come. Just don't forget the rag snips!

materials

makes a 55" X 64" layer cake quilt

QUILT TOP
• 2 flannel layer cakes

EXTRAS
• Rag Quilt Snips by Fiskars

SAMPLE QUILT
• **Woolies Flannels** by Maywood Studios

1 pair & sew

Pair up 2 layer cakes of the same print WST (wrong sides together). Stitch across diagonally from corner to corner twice, making an X. Repeat for all pairs.

Yield: 42 blocks

2 arrange & sew

Lay out all the blocks in a 6 x 7 grid setting. The goal is to achieve an even mix of lights and darks throughout.

Sew blocks together with a ½" seam through all 4 layers of fabric. Keep all seam allowances facing up on the same side of the quilt. **2B**

1 pair 2 same print layer cakes wrong sides together; stitch diagonally across corner to corner

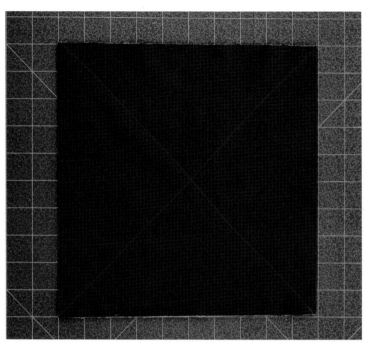

1 Sew 2 lines of stitching across a pair of layer cakes paired up wrong sides together. See step 1.

2 Sew blocks together with ½″ seam allowances. There will be 4 layers of fabric. See 2B

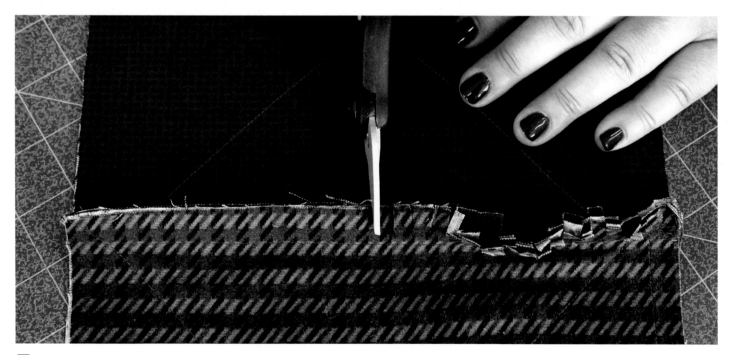

3 Using rag snips cut into the seam allowances. Keep back from the stitching line. See step 4.

Build rows first. Then sew rows together.

Quilt size: 55" x 64"

3 outside edge

Stitch around the entire outside perimeter ½" inch from the edge.

4 rag the seams

Clip into all 4 layers of the seam allowances at about ⅜" intervals. Clip up to the line of stitching but not through it. Using a pair of rag scissors will save your hands from strain.

Clip the outside edge of the quilt as well—and you're done!

2A sew 2 blocks together to build a row

2B stitch through 4 layers using a ½" seam allowance; all seam allowances face the same side

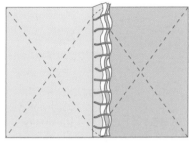

4 clip the seam allowances . . .

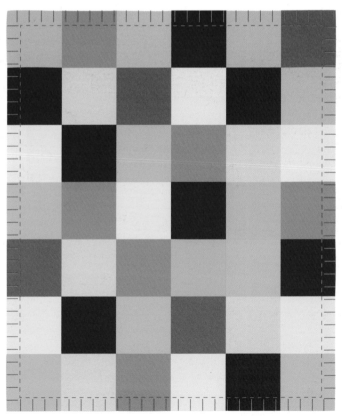

4 . . . and the outside perimeter

Big Wonky Star

designed by NATALIE EARNHEART

When I was ten years old, I desperately wanted to learn how to sew. My mother was not a seamstress by any stretch of the imagination, so I knew I was going to have to look elsewhere for instruction. Finally, I decided to join the local 4-H club and my love affair with needle and thread began.

Our club started with a few simple projects. I remember making my own apron and I loved every moment. From there I went on to sew several items of clothing and soon I was completely hooked!

When constructing clothing, you get used to following patterns and directions. But I've never really been content to just color inside the lines. Every time I started a new

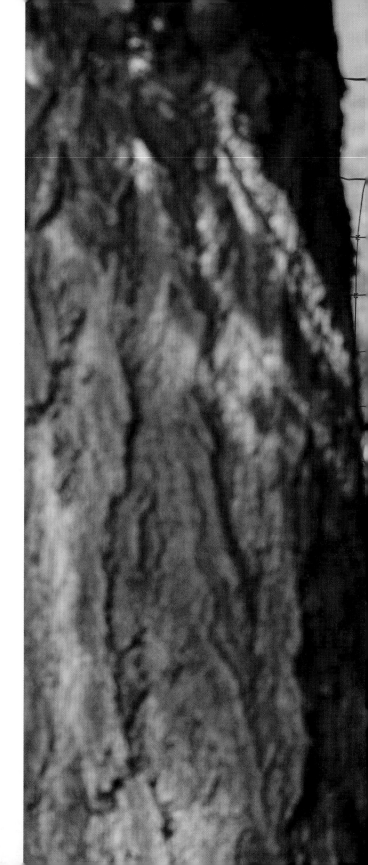

I CHERISH THE MEMORIES I HAVE of quilting with my friends. Friendship is like a patchwork quilt of caring words, thoughtful deeds, and lots of laughter, all stitched together with love and understanding.

project, my mind would run wild with ideas of how I could change this or that to really make it my own. I'd start with a dress pattern that I liked, but then I'd use a different style of sleeve or alter the neckline, add a bow, change a seam, etc. Pretty soon I'd have a wonderful dress that looked almost nothing like the pattern!

Like many of you, when I was first introduced to quilting, the thing that I loved the most was the creative freedom. I loved being able to make little changes here and there to design a whole new pattern. As I became more experienced at constructing blocks and fitting all the pieces together, I just couldn't stop thinking of ways that I could make things simpler and more beautiful. Quilting becam such an important artistic outlet for me; I was able to express my ideas and emotions through quilting as freely as a painter does on canvas.

And yet as much as I have always treasured the creative freedom of quilting, when I was introduced to the Wonky Star, it made me feel a little uneasy. It was just so out of the box—so against the grain of everything I had done before. I wondered if I would really be able to quilt in such an unconventional and free-spirited way.

Finally, I decided to just jump in and give it my best effort, and to my surprise, I absolutely loved it! It was so freeing and fun, and despite the lack of traditional construction, it just worked, and it looked great! The Wonky Star is designed to be unique and personalized to the individual quilter. It really forces you to take charge of your own design and maybe walk outside of your comfort zone. But for me, it's a risk well worth taking!

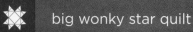

materials

makes a 58" X 67½" layer cake quilt

QUILT TOP
- 1 print layer cake
- 1 yd solid for stars

BINDING
- ½ yd coordinating fabric

BACKING
- 3¾ yds coordinating fabric

SAMPLE QUILT
- **Fancy Free** by Lori Whitlock for Riley Blake
- **Optical White** by RJR

1 cut

From the star fabric, cut:
   (3) 10" strips;
     Subcut into (12) 10" squares

2 arrange

Lay out the print layer cakes in a 6 x 7 setting. Try for a balance of lights and darks. Remove 3 squares and replace them with 3 solid star squares. The blocks bordering the sides of the star squares will be getting star legs in the next step.

3 create a star leg

Fingerpress a small fold on one side of a print layer cake marking the halfway point.

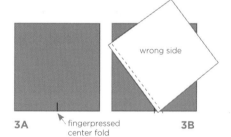

3A   fingerpressed center fold   3B

wrong side

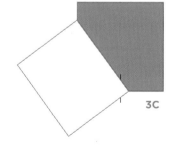

3C

3A fingerpress center;
3B lay the solid star LC on an angle crossing the center fold; sew ¼" seam;
3C flip & press

1 Position the first star leg at an angle making sure to cross over the center point of one side. See 3B

2 Trim the star leg fabric to the background square. Save as large a piece as possible for the next star leg. 3D & E

3 Open the star leg and trim excess print fabric along the leg's edge. 3F

4 The second star leg is created with trimmed fabric from 3D/E. Its seam will cross the first leg at least ¼" above the block's edge. 4A

5 Press into place. Trim off the excess fabric using the print layer cake as a template as before. 4B

6 Remove excess print fabric from behind the second star leg.

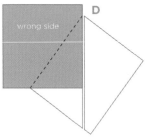
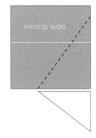

3D-F trim star leg

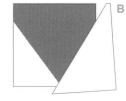
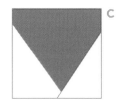

4 second star leg

With RST position a 10″ solid square at an angle to make the first leg of the star. Overlap the halfway point fold. Sew a ¼″ seam along the edge of the white star fabric. Flip and press out. **3A-C**

To trim, turn the block upside down and remove excess fabric using the background square as the cutting guide. Make 2 cuts **3D** & **3E**.

Flip the block to the front, open the star leg and trim excess bulk underneath. Leave a ¼″ seam allowance. **3F**

4 second star leg

Use the larger scrap piece from **3B** to create the second star point. Place it RST crossing over the first star leg at or above ¼″ seam allowance. The red dot indicates ¼.″ Make sure the piece will cover the corner of the print layer cake before sewing. **4A** Sew. Press open. **4B** Flip to the back and trim to the background square as in **3B-C**. Flip to the front, trim excess fabric as in **3D**. Make 9 star leg blocks. **4C**

Block size: 10″ x 10″

5 quilt center

Reposition the star leg blocks next to their star centers. Follow the diagram. Build rows by sewing blocks together across. Press seams to the same side in a row; to the opposite side in the next row. Then sew rows together, nesting seams as you go.

6 quilt & bind

Layer quilt top on batting and backing and quilt the way you like. Square up all raw edges.

Cut (8) 2½″ strips from binding fabric to finish. See *construction basics* for greater detail.

7 quilt & bind

Layer quilt top on batting and backing and quilt the way you like. Square up all raw edges.

Cut (8) 2½″ strips from binding fabric to finish. See *construction basics* for greater detail.

How to piece your batting

Don't you love it when you put your fabric scraps to good use? We love that feeling too! It's so fun to take "leftovers" and turn them into something great! We love to use up our batting scraps just as much!

Sometimes we just want to use up small pieces. Other times we have a quilt that is just too large for the standard batting sizes and needs its batting to be augmented. Either way, piecing batting is a great option. We recommend only piecing 2-3 pieces per quilt, just to be safe.

Here is what to do. First square up your batting scraps. You want to make sure that your edges are straight so that they will meet together in a neat line. You can get a nice straight edge by overlapping the edges that you will be joining and cutting through both layers. Remove any excess.

Next, you will want to join these pieces. There are several ways to do this. All of these will start with lining up your batting pieces next to each other. To prevent a lumpy seam, make sure the batting doesn't overlap. The two batting pieces should just sit side by side. Then comes the bond. Here are 3 methods of joining batting:

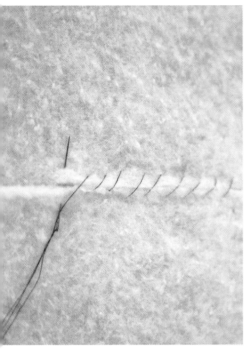

One way is to hand-stitch the batting scraps together using a basic ladder or whip stitch. Keep your stitches close together and spaced evenly. Use thread that matches your batting so it's as invisible as possible.

Another way is to machine stitch using a large zig zag. It just needs to be wide enough to catch both batting pieces and long enough to prevent your batting from ruffling or bunching up. Be sure to keep your pieces lined up side by side as you run it through your machine.

You could also use a strip of heat activated stabilizer or batting tape to fuse the pieces together. Again, line up your batting side by side, lay the stabilizer or batting tape over the seam and press with a hot iron until the seam is fused.

All of these methods work beautifully, and once quilted they are invisible to the eye and very sturdy. Try it out, and let us know what you think!

How to sew a cuddle scarf

When the leaves start to change and the temperatures drop, a scarf can be your new best friend. It warms your neck and adds a touch of style to your outfit. It can be that pop of color or add a touch of elegance to dress up your ensemble. These cuddle infinity scarves are a perfect blend of warmth and style, and they are a snap to make. Plus, when you get three scarves from a yard of fabric, you can't beat the price! We make them for our friends, our kids, their friends and teachers. Everyone loves these scarves. They look great on men, women, and kids. And once you see the selection of fabrics available you'll want them all!

1 cut
Cut 1 yard of cuddle cloth into (3) 12" x 60" rectangles.

Yield: (3) 12" x 60"

2 sew
Fold a rectangle in half lengthwise RST (right sides together) and sew the raw edges together. You now have a tube.

3 do the twist
Turn the tube right side out. Twist one end 3 times.

1 3 times: 12" x 60"

raw edges

fold

2 fold in half lengthwise and sew raw edges together

3 turn right sides out; twist 3 times

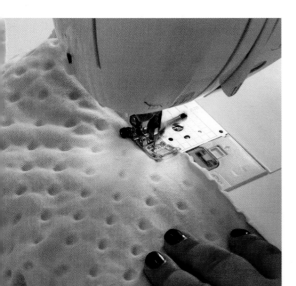

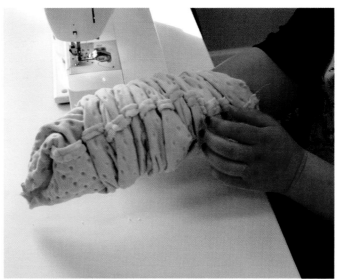

materials

YARDAGE
1 yard cuddle cloth

SAMPLE SCARF
Cuddle Cloth by
Shannon Fabrics

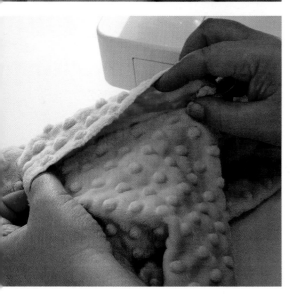

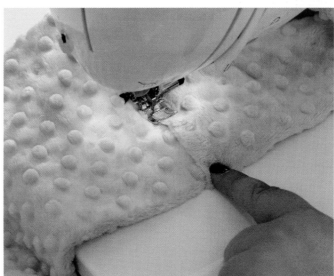

4 finishing

Tuck one raw edge of the tube inside the other.
Match seams and sew across through all layers
at once.

Yield: 1 cuddle scarf

Make 3 total

Wear like a goddess!

4   tuck one raw end inside the other end;
    match up the seams; stitch across

big wonky star

QUILT SIZE
58" X 67½"

DESIGNED BY
Natalie Earnheart

PIECED BY
Natalie Earnheart

QUILTED BY
Cassie Martin

QUILT TOP
1 print layer cake
1 yd solid for stars

BINDING
½ yd coordinating fabric

BACKING
3¾ yds coordinating fabric

SAMPLE QUILT
Fancy Free by Lori Whitlock for Riley Blake
Optical White by RJR

ONLINE TUTORIALS
msqc.co/bigwonkystar

QUILTING
Curly Twirly Flowers

QUILT PATTERN
pg 74

 TIP: *Want to make a different size? No problem, check out these and other patterns online!*

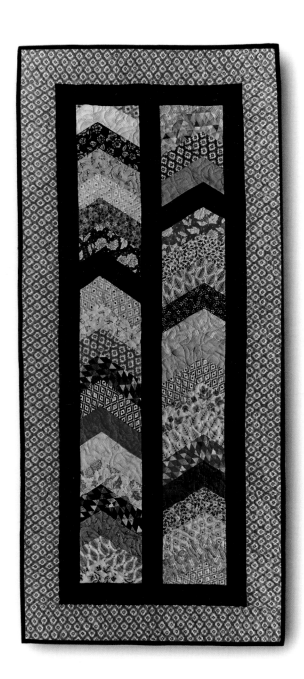

hexagon braid

TABLE TOP RUNNER SIZE
24½″ X 52½″

DESIGNED BY
Natalie Earnheart

PIECED BY
Cassie Nixdorf

QUILTED BY
Betty Bates

TABLE TOP RUNNER TOP
1 print 5″ square pack
½ yd solid for sashing/inner border
½ yd outer border

BINDING
½ yd coordinating fabric

BACKING
1¾ yds coordinating fabric

SAMPLE TABLE RUNNER
Persimmon by BasicGrey for Moda Fabrics

ONLINE TUTORIALS
msqc.co/hexagonbraid

QUILTING
Fall Leaves

PATTERN
pg 24

jelly roll
race 3

QUILT SIZE
66½" X 77½"

DESIGNED BY
Jenny Doan

PIECED BY
Stephen Nixdorf

QUILTED BY
Mari Zullig

QUILT TOP
1 jelly roll
1 yd solid for inner border
& triangles
1¼ yds outer border

BINDING
¾ yd coordinating fabric

BACKING
4¼ yds 45" wide
OR 2¼ yds 90" wide

SAMPLE QUILT
Lily's Garden Spice
by Patrick Lose for RJR
Cream by Cotton Supremes
for RJR

ONLINE TUTORIAL
msqc.co/jellyrollrace3

QUILTING
G'Daisy

QUILT PATTERN
pg 40

rag quilt

QUILT SIZE
55" X 64"

DESIGNED BY
Jenny Doan

PIECED BY
Cassie Nixdorf

QUILT TOP
2 flannel layer cakes

EXTRAS
Rag Quilt Snips by Fiskars

SAMPLE QUILT
Woolies Flannels
by Maywood Studios

ONLINE TUTORIALS
msqc.co/rag

QUILT PATTERN
pg 66

serendipity I

QUILT SIZE
58" X 64"

DESIGNED BY
Jenny Doan

PIECED BY
Natalie Earnheart

QUILTED BY
Amber Wendt

QUILT TOP
1 print jelly roll
2½ yds background fabric
1 yd outer border

BINDING
½ yd coordinating fabric

BACKING
3¾ yds coordinating fabric

SAMPLE QUILT
Singapore Sling
by Stonehenge for Northcott
Studio
Stonehenge Cream
by Stonehenge for Northcott
Studio

ONLINE TUTORIALS
msqc.co/serendipity1

QUILTING
Simple Stipple

QUILT PATTERN
PG 48

serendipity II

QUILT SIZE
55" X 55"

DESIGNED BY
Jenny Doan

PIECED BY
Natalie Earnheart

QUILTED BY
Mari Zullig

QUILT TOP
(144) 4½" cast off blocks
¾ yd outer border

BINDING
½ yd coordinating fabric

BACKING
3½ yds coordinating fabric

SAMPLE QUILT
Singapore Sling
by Stonehenge for Northcott
Studio
Stonehenge Cream
by Stonehenge for Northcott
Studio

ONLINE TUTORIALS
msqc.co/serendipity2

QUILTING
Dense Leaves

PATTERN
PG 56

sidewalk chalk

QUILT SIZE
106" x 90"

DESIGNED BY
Natalie Earnheart

PIECED BY
Natalie Earnheart

QUILTED BY
Daniela Kirk

QUILT TOP
1 print jelly roll
2 yds solid background
3¼ yds white background
1½ yds outer border

BINDING
¾ yd coordinating fabric

BACKING
8¼ yds **OR** 3¼ yds 108" wide

SAMPLE QUILT
Glow by Amy Butler for Rowan
Bella Breeze (132) by Moda
Fabrics
Bella Solids White (98) by
Moda Fabrics

ONLINE TUTORIALS
msqc.co/sidewalkchalk

QUILTING
Posies

QUILT PATTERN
PG 58

snowballed pinwheel

QUILT SIZE
50" X 60½"

DESIGNED BY
Natalie Earnheart

PIECED BY
Cassie Nixdorf

QUILTED BY
Sam Earnheart

QUILT TOP
2 print charm packs
4 solid charm packs
¾ yd outer border

BINDING
½ yd coordinating fabric

BACKING
3¼ yds coordinating fabric

SAMPLE QUILT
Rambling Rose by Sandy Gervais
for Moda Fabrics
Bella Solids Snow (11) by Moda
Fabrics

ONLINE TUTORIALS
msqc.co/snowballedpin

QUILTING
Meandering Flower

QUILT PATTERN
PG 8

TIP: *Want to make a different size? No problem, check out these and other patterns online!*

teacup

QUILT SIZE
68" X 76½"

DESIGNED BY
Natalie Earnheart

PIECED BY
Cassie Nixdorf

QUILTED BY
Jamey Stone

QUILT TOP
1 print layer cake
½ yd inner border
1½ yds outer border

BINDING
½ yd coordinating fabric

BACKING
4¼ yds **OR** 2¼ yds 90" wide

SAMPLE QUILT
French Navy by Studio 8
for Quilting Treasures

ONLINE TUTORIALS
msqc.co/teacup

QUILTING
Flower Swirls

QUILT PATTERN
PG 16

triangle tango

QUILT SIZE
113" X 97"

DESIGNED BY
Natalie Earnheart

PIECED BY
Natalie Earnheart

QUILTED BY
Emma Jensen

QUILT TOP
1 print layer cake
1 solid layer cake
5 yds solid yardage
OR 2 solid jelly rolls (same solid
as the layer cakes)

BINDING
1 yd coordinating fabric

BACKING
8¾ yds **OR** 3½ yds 108" wide

SAMPLE QUILT
Moonshine by Tula Pink for Free
Spirit Fabrics
Arctic White by Free Spirit
Fabrics

ONLINE TUTORIALS
msqc.co/triangletango

QUILTING
Loops & Swirls

QUILT PATTERN
pg 32

general guidelines

- All seams are ¼" inch unless directions specify differently.

- Cutting instructions are given at the point when cutting is required.

- Precuts are not prewashed; therefore do not prewash other fabrics in the project

- All strips are cut WOF

- Remove all selvages

- All yardages based on 42" WOF

ACRONYMS USED

MSQC	Missouri Star Quilt Co.
RST	right sides together
WST	wrong sides together
HST	half square triangle
WOF	width of fabric
LOF	length of fabric

pre-cut glossary

CHARM PACK
1 = (42) 5" squares or ¾ yd of fabric
1 = baby
2 = crib
3 = lap
4 = twin

JELLY ROLL
1 = (40) 2½" strips cut the width of fabric
    or 2¾ yds of fabric
1 = a twin
2 = queen

LAYER CAKE
1 = (42) 10" squares of fabric: 2¾ yds total
1 = a twin
2 = queen

The terms charm pack, jelly roll, and layer cake are trademarked names that belong to Moda. Other companies use different terminology, but the sizes remain the same.

When we mention a precut, we are basing the pattern on a 40-42 count pack. Not all precuts have the same count, so be sure to check the count on your precut to make sure you have enough pieces to complete your project.

press seams

- Use a steam iron on the cotton setting.

- Iron the seam just as it was sewn RST. This "sets" the seam.

- With dark fabric on top, lift the dark fabric and press back.

- The seam allowance is pressed to the dark side. Some patterns may direct otherwise for certain situations.

- Follow pressing arrows in the diagrams when indicated.

- Press toward borders. Pieced borders may demand otherwise.

- Press diagonal seams open on binding to reduce bulk.

binding

- Use 2½" strips for binding.

- Sew strips end-to-end into one long strip with diagonal seams, aka plus sign method (next). Press seams open.

- Fold in half lengthwise WST and press.

- The entire length should equal the outside dimension of the quilt plus 15" - 20."

plus sign method

Diagonal seams are used when straight seams would add too much bulk.

- Lay one strip across the other as if to make a plus sign RST.

- Sew from top inside to bottom outside corners crossing the intersections of fabric as you sew. Trim excess to ¼" seam allowance.

- Press seam open.

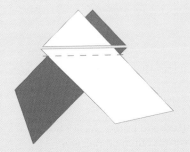

wrong side

attach binding

- Match raw edges of folded binding to the quilt top edge.
- Leave a 10″ tail at the beginning.
- Use a ¼″ seam allowance.
- Start in the middle of a long straight side.

miter binding corners

- Stop sewing ¼″ before the corner.
- Move the quilt out from under the pressure foot.
- Clip the threads.
- Flip the binding up at a 90˚ angle to the edge just sewn.
- Fold the binding down along the next side to be sewn.
- Align the fold to the edge of the quilt that was *just sewn*;
- Align raw edges to the side *to be sewn*.
- Begin sewing on the fold.

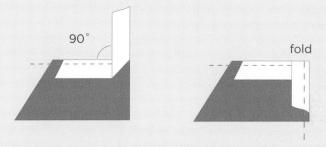

close binding

MSQC recommends **The Binding Tool** *from TQM Products to finish binding perfectly every time.*

- Stop sewing when you have 12″ left to reach the start.
- Where the binding tails come together trim excess leaving only 2½″ of overlap.
- It helps to pin or clip the quilt together at the two points where the binding starts and stops. This takes the pressure off of the binding tails while you work.
- Use the plus sign method to sew the two binding ends together, except this time when making the plus sign, match the edges. Using a pencil mark your sewing line since you won't be able to see where the corners intersect. Sew across.
- Trim off excess; press seam open.
- Fold in half WST and align all raw edges to the quilt top.
- Sew this last binding section to the quilt. Press.
- Turn the folded edge of the binding around to the back of the quilt and tack into place with an invisible stitch or machine stitch if you wish.

borders

- Always measure the quilt center 3 times before cutting borders.
- Start with the width and measure the top edge, middle and bottom.
- Folding the quilt in half is a quick way to find the middle.
- Take the average of those 3 measurements.
- Cut 2 border strips to that size.
- Attach one to the top; one to the bottom of the quilt.
- Position the border fabric on top as you sew. The feed dogs can act like rufflers. Having the border on top will prevent waviness and keep the quilt straight.
- Repeat this process for the side borders, measuring the length 3 times.
- Include the newly attached top and bottom borders in your measurements.
- Press to the borders.

PATCHWORK MURDER

PART 4
Mystery Quilt

——— A JENNY DOAN MYSTERY ———

written by Steve Westover

After tucking MK in for a much needed rest, Jenny called her husband and MK's mom to share the harrowing experience. She then returned to room 409. The police presence had diminished but Detective Scanlan stood in front of the yellow police tape with a smirk as Brubeck stormed away.

"You two have a sweet relationship," Jenny quipped. If Scanlan was amused he didn't show it. Realizing no response was forthcoming she continued. "You're not one of those cliché tough-guy cops with no people skills, are you?"

"What do you want Mrs. Doan?" he asked.

"OK, so you are. Disappointing." Jenny straightened her posture. "I can act official too." No response. "All-righty, what I'm really wanting is my bag; clothes, makeup and my presentation materials."

"Sorry, Mrs. Doan. No can do. It's evidence. We'll get it back to you when we're finished."

"And when will that be? Tomorrow?"

Detective Scanlan laughed out loud. "Not a chance. A couple of weeks...if you're lucky."

"What exactly do you think you'll find in there? A cute top?" Jenny questioned.

"I can't really know that, can I? That's why everything has to be examined," Scanlan said. "The victim and his mystery partner stole the bags for a reason."

Everything Scanlan said was reasonable and Jenny felt a twinge of guilt for caring more about her bag than about Scanlan's investigation. Even Bruno deserved better than murder.

If Bruno hadn't helped to hide MK she could also be lying on a slab at the morgue. "Look, Detective Scanlan, when we figure out the reason for the theft we'll uncover the motive for murder."

Detective Scanlan's jaw tightened and his face turned red. "'We?' You have nothing to do with this investigation Mrs. Doan. You will stay out of my way. Do you understand?"

"I liked you so much better an hour ago," Jenny muttered. "No, I don't understand. This has everything to do with me. Not only am I a victim but MK's a witness." Scanlan tried to speak but Jenny waved him off. "In fact, the murderer could still be in this hotel. What if he didn't find what he was looking for?" The words raced so quickly she could hardly believe they were hers. Jenny thought for a moment. "What if they didn't steal the right bags? What if there's another quilter at risk? What if the killer realizes there was a witness?" Fear enveloped Jenny as she pondered her last question.

Scanlan sighed and motioned his hands downward as if to say, "calm down." He immediately realized the rudeness of his gesture and tried to make amends. His voice softened and his Midwest drawl made an encore appearance. "Mrs. Doan, there are quilters everywhere." He motioned to a white haired woman walking past them with a patchwork sewing bag hanging from her shoulder. He lowered his voice. "No one's trying to kill quilters."

Jenny smiled, recognizing she had the upper hand. "Really? How can you be so sure? Have you somehow surmised the motive in the last 60 seconds?" Scanlan stumbled as he searched for words but Jenny knew he couldn't defend the statement. "These are my people," Jenny said. "I can help you."

"Impossible," Detective Scanlan said. "Like you said, you're too involved. I couldn't put you at risk and frankly, I don't need your help."

Jenny glared at the unkempt detective and nodded as she considered her next move. Scanlan was right. Quilters packed every nook of the hotel. How could he possibly find a potential victim in this group? Then Jenny had an idea. She remembered how Bruno had been waiting for another passenger at the airport terminal. Why did he wait? He wasn't a real shuttle driver. Only one answer came to Jenny's mind. He must have been waiting for that final passenger. Jenny tried to recall the final